URDU

FOR BEGINNERS

FIRST 1000 WORDS

EFFIE DELAROSA

CONTENTS

CONTENTS

CONTENTS

ہاں جی
Han

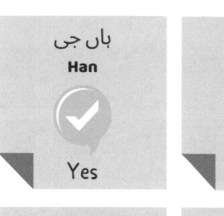

Yes

نہیں
Nahi

No

ہیلو
Hello

Hello

شکریہ
Shukria

Thank You

خدا حافظ
Khuda Hafiz

Goodbye

براہ مہربانی
Brahe Meharbani

Please

اور
Aur

And

یا
Ya

Or

یہ
Yeh

This

میں
Mein

I

تُم
Tum

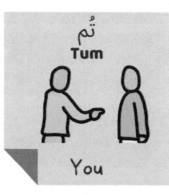

You

وُہ (مذکر)
Woh (Male)

He

وُہ (مؤنث)
Woh (Female)

She

ہم
Hum

We

وُہ (ایک سے زیادہ)
Woh (more than one)

They

معذرت
Mazrat

Sorry

لیکن
Lekin

But

شام بخیر
Sham bakhair

Good evening

کیونکہ
Kiunkeh

Because

خوش آمدید
Khush aamdeed

Welcome

کہاں
Kahan

Where

کیا
Kia

What

کتنا
Kitna

How much

کونسا
Konsa

Which

زبردست
Zabardast

Awesome

پیارا
Pyara

Cute

مدد
Madad

Help

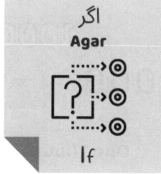

اگر
Agar

If

کب
Kab

When

کیوں
Kiun

Why

اعداد

ADAAD

NUMBERS

0 Sifar Zero	1 Aik One	2 Do Two
3 Teen Three	4 Char Four	5 Paanch Five
6 Chhe Six	7 Saat Seven	8 Aath Eight
9 No Nine	10 Das Ten	15 Pandrah Fifteen
20 Bees Twenty	100 So One Hundred	1000 Hazar One Thousand

خاندان
KHANDAN

FAMILY

والدہ
Walida
Mother

والد
Waalid
Father

بھائی
Bhai
Brother

بہن
Behan
Sister

دادی
Daadi
Grandma

دادا
Dada
Grandpa

بیٹا
Beta
Son

بیٹی
Beti
Daughter

چچی / خالہ
Chachi / Khala
Aunt

چچا
Chacha
Uncle

پوتی / نواسی
Poti/Nawasi
Granddaughter

پوتا / نواسا
Pota/Nawasa
Grandson

بیوی
Biwi
Wife

خاوند
Khavand
Husband

ناشتہ
Nashta
Breakfast

دوپہر کا کھانا
Dopahar ka khana
Lunch

ڈبل روٹی
Double Roti
Bread

رات کا کھانا
Raat ka khana
Dinner

کھانا
Khana
Meal

پنیر
Paneer
Cheese

انڈا
Anda
Egg

مچھلی
Machli
Fish

گوشت
Gosht
Meat

مکھن
Makhan
Butter

ران کا ٹکڑا
Raan ka Tukra
Ham

ساسیج
Sausage
Sausage

دہی
Dahi
Yogurt

کیک
Cake
Cake

چاکلیٹ
Chocolate
Chocolate

نمک
Namak
Salt

چینی
Cheeni
Sugar

آٹا
Aata
Flour

کالی مرچ
Kaali mirch
Pepper

ڈرنک
Drink
Drink

لالی پاپ
Lollipop
Lollipop

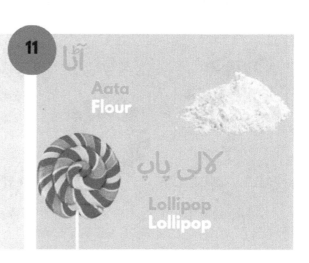

شہد
Shehad
Honey

ڈونٹ
Dawnat
Doughnut

پانی
Paani
Water

کافی
Coffee
Coffee

آئس کریم
Ice Cream
Ice Cream

دودھ
Doodh
Milk

مالٹے کا جوس
Maltay ka juice
Orange Juice

چائے
Chai
Tea

باٹ چاکلیٹ
Hot chocolate
Hot Chocolate

خوراک
Khoraak
Food

حیاتین
Hayaateen
Vitamin

پیاز
Pyaaz
Onion

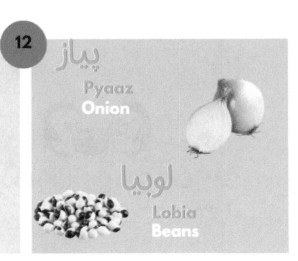

میٹھی ڈش
Meethi Dish
Dessert

اناج
Anaj
Cereals

لوبیا
Lobia
Beans

مکئی
Makai
Corn

گندم
Gandum
Wheat

جوُ
Jo
Oat

ٹماٹر کی چٹنی
Timatar ki chatni
Ketchup

سرسوں
Sarson
Mustard

مصالحہ جات
Masalha jaat
Spices

تیل
Tail
Oil

چاول
Chawal
Rice

پاستا
Pasta
Pasta

سواریاں
sawarian

vehicles

ہوائی جہاز	کشتی	جہاز
HAWAI JAHAAZ	**KASHTI**	**JAHAAZ**
AIRPLANE	BOAT	SHIP

گاڑی	موٹر سائیکل	ریل گاڑی
GAARI	**MOTORCYCLE**	**RAIL GAARI**
CAR	MOTORBIKE	TRAIN

ٹریکٹر	سائیکل	بس
TRACKTOR	**CYCLE**	**BUS**
TRACTOR	BICYCLE	BUS

کرائے کی گاڑی	سب وے	ٹرک
KIRAYE KI GAARI	**SUBWAY**	**TRUCK**
TAXI	SUBWAY	TRUCK

ایمبولینس	بیلی کاپٹر	ٹرام
AMBULANCE	**HELICOPTER**	**TRAM**
AMBULANCE	HELICOPTER	TRAM

سفر
safar

travel

14

چھٹی	بوائی اڈہ	ٹرین سٹیشن
CHUTTI	**HAWAI ADDA**	**TRAIN STAESHAN**
HOLIDAY	AIRPORT	TRAIN STATION

بندرگاہ	سیاح	ہوٹل
BANDAR GAH	**SAYAH**	**HOTEL**
PORT	TOURIST	HOTEL

گھر	اپارٹمنٹ	سُوٹ کیس
GHAR	**APARTMENT**	**SUITCASE**
HOUSE	APARTMENT	SUITCASE

پاسپورٹ	نقشہ	سوئمنگ پول
PASSPORT	**NAQSHA**	**SWIMMING POL**
PASSPORT	MAP	SWIMMING POOL

سڑک	گلی	سیر
SARHAK	**GALI**	**SAIR**
ROAD	STREET	WALK

پرندہ
Parinda

Bird

بلی
Billi

Cat

کتا
Kutta

Dog

بطخ
Batakh

Duck

چوہا
Chooha

Mouse

کبوتر
Kabootar

Pigeon

خرگوش
Khargosh

Rabbit

ہاتھی
Haathi

Elephant

بندر
Bandar

Monkey

مرغی
Murghi

Chicken

گائے
Gaaye

Cow

گدھا
Gadha

Donkey

بکری
Bakri

Goat

گھوڑا
Ghoraa

Horse

سور
Soor

Pig

جانور

JANWAR

ANIMALS

بھیڑ
Bheer

Sheep

ہنس
Hanss

Goose

ریچھ
Reechh

Bear

اونٹ
Oont

Camel

مینڈک
Mayndak

Frog

سانپ
Saanp

Snake

کچھوا
Kachwa

Turtle

بھیڑیا
Bheyrya

Wolf

مگرمچھ
Magarmach

Crocodile

ڈائیناسور
Dina Saur

Dinosaur

زرافہ
Ziraafa

Giraffe

کینگرو
Kangaroo

Kangaroo

چھپکلی
Chipkali

Lizard

چیتا
Cheeta

Tiger

زیبرا
Zebra

Zebra

جانور

JANWAR

ANIMALS

شارک
Shark

Shark

کیکڑا
Kekra

Crab

ڈالفن
Dolphin

Dolphin

جیلی فش
Jellyfish

Jellyfish

جھینگا مچھلی
Jheenga Machhli

Lobster

سمندری گھوڑا
Samandari Ghora

Seahorse

رے
Ray

Ray

آکٹوپس
Octopus

Octopus

تتلی
Titli

Butterfly

لال بیگ
Lal bag

Cockroach

مکڑی
Makri

Spider

بیٹل
Beetle

Beetle

بھنبھیری
Bhinbhri

Dragonfly

چیونٹی
Choonti

Ant

شہد کی مکھی
Shehad Ki Makhi

Bee

جانور

JANWAR

ANIMALS

دن / DIN — DAY

پیر / PEER	منگل / MANGAL	بدھ / BUDH	جمعرات / JUME-RAAT
MONDAY	TUESDAY	WEDNESDAY	THURSDAY

جمعہ / JUMMA	ہفتہ / HAFTA	اتوار / ITWAAR	ہفتہ / HAFTA
FRIDAY	SATURDAY	SUNDAY	WEEK

وقت / WAQT — TIME

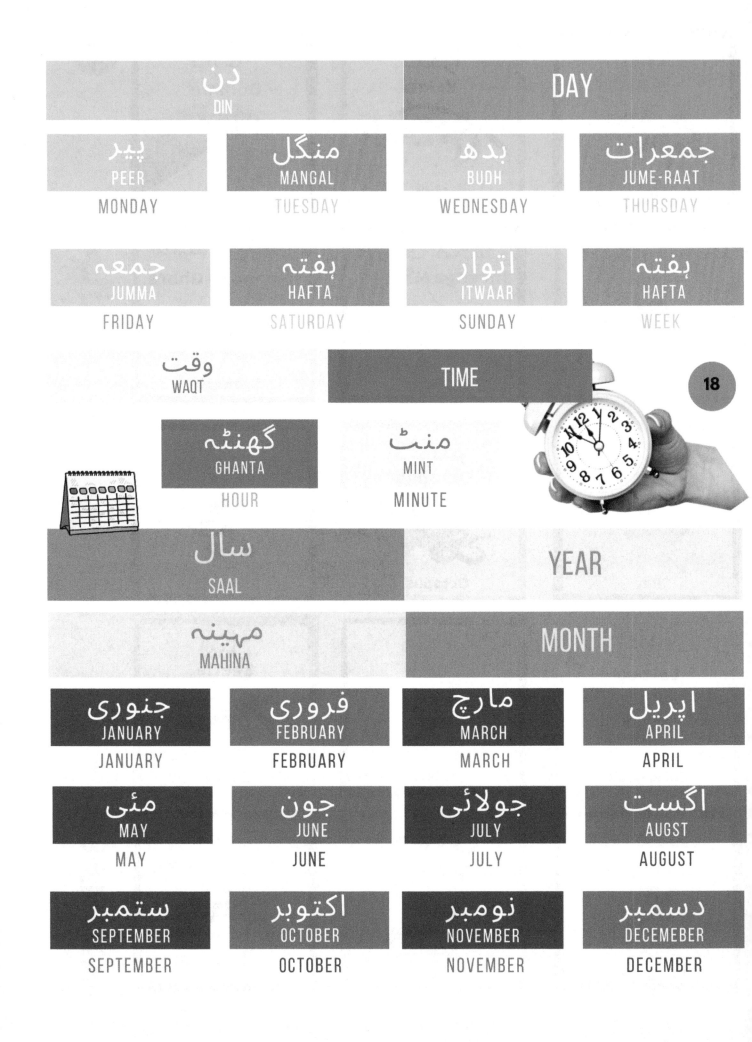

گھنٹہ / GHANTA	منٹ / MINT
HOUR	MINUTE

سال / SAAL — YEAR

مہینہ / MAHINA — MONTH

جنوری / JANUARY	فروری / FEBRUARY	مارچ / MARCH	اپریل / APRIL
JANUARY	FEBRUARY	MARCH	APRIL

مئی / MAY	جون / JUNE	جولائی / JULY	اگست / AUGST
MAY	JUNE	JULY	AUGUST

ستمبر / SEPTEMBER	اکتوبر / OCTOBER	نومبر / NOVEMBER	دسمبر / DECEMEBER
SEPTEMBER	OCTOBER	NOVEMBER	DECEMBER

18

موسم سرما
Jara
Mosam Sarma

بہار
Baahar
Spring

موسم
Mosam
Season

خزان
Khizan
Autumn

موسم گرما
Mosam Garma
Summer

ہوا
Hawa
Wind

بارش
Barish
Rain

طوفان
Tofan
Thunderstorm

صبح
Subah
Morning

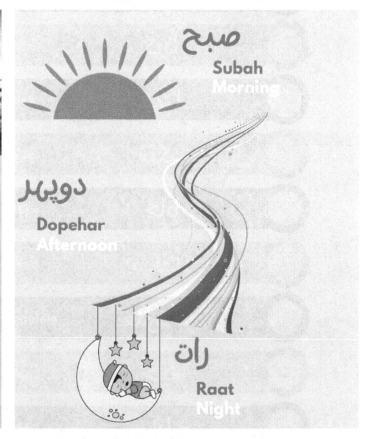

دوپہر
Dopehar
Afternoon

رات
Raat
Night

آب و ہوا
Aabo hawa
Climate

حال
Hal
Present

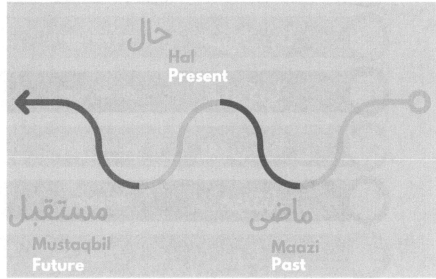

مستقبل
Mustaqbil
Future

ماضی
Maazi
Past

فعل
FAIL

VERBS

پاس ہونا	pas hona	have
ہونا	hona	be
کرنا	karna	do
کہنا	kehna	say
سکنا	sakna	can
جانا	jana	go
دیکھنا	dekhna	see
معلوم ہونا	maloom hona	know
چاہنا	chahna	want
آنا	aana	come
ضرورت ہونا	zaroorat hona	need
ضرور کرنا	zaroor hona	have to
یقین کرنا	yaqeen karna	believe
ڈھونڈنا	dhoondna	find
دینا	dena	give

لینا	layna	take
بولنا	bolna	talk
رکھنا	rakhna	put
دکھائی دینا	dikhayi daina	seem
چھوڑنا	chorna	leave
رہنا	rahna	stay
سوچنا	sochna	think
دیکھنا	dekhna	look
جواب دینا	jawab daina	answer
انتظار کرنا	intezar karna	wait
زندہ ہونا	zinda hona	live
سمجھنا	samjhna	understand
اندر آنا	andar aana	come in
بن جانا	ban jana	become
واپس آنا	wapis aana	come back

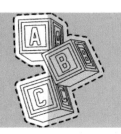

لکھنا	likhna	write
طلب کرنا	talabb karna	call
گرنا	girna	fall
شروع کرنا	shuro karna	start
پیروی کرنا	pairwi karna	follow
دکھانا	dikhana	show
ہنسنا	hasna	laugh
مسکرانا	muskurana	smile
یاد رکھنا	yaad rakhna	remember
کھیلنا	khailna	play
کھانا	khana	eat
پڑھنا	parhna	read
حاصل کرنا	hasil karna	get
رونا	rona	cry
سمجھانا	samjhana	explain

گانا	gaana	sing
چھونا	chona	touch
سونگھنا	songhna	smell
سانس لینا	sans lena	breathe
سننا	sunna	hear
رنگ کرنا	rangna	paint
مطالعہ کرنا	mutalea karna	study
جشن منانا	jashan manana	celebrate
منتخب کریں	muntakhib karna	choose
تلاش کرنا	talash karna	search
پوچھنا	pochna	ask
لطف اٹھانا	lutf uthana	enjoy
تصور کرنا	tasawwur karna	imagine
پینا	peena	drink
تبدیل کرنا	tabdeel karna	change

حروف
Huroof
Alphabet

کاپی
Copy
Notebook

پنسل
Pencil
Pencil

اسکول کا بستہ
School ka basta
Schoolbag

قینچی
Qainchi
Scissors

طالب علم
Taalib E Ilm
Student

کلاس روم
Classroom
Classroom

دوست
Dost
Friends

پروفیسر
Professor
Professor

ریاضی
Riazi
Mathematics

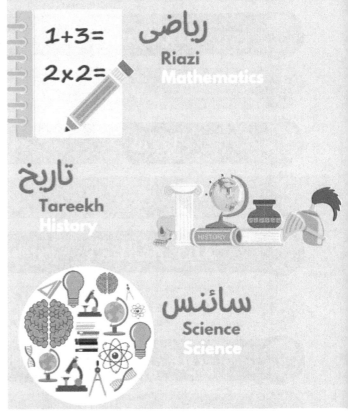

تاریخ
Tareekh
History

سائنس
Science
Science

اسکول
School
School

آرٹس
Arts
Arts

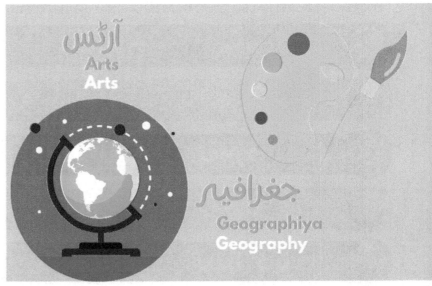

جغرافیہ
Geographiya
Geography

ملازمت
mulazmat

job

نرس
NURSE
NURSE

كسان
KISAN
FARMER

معمار
MAMAAR
ARCHITECT

انجينير
ENGINEER
ENGINEER

مزدور
MAZDOR
LABORER

فائر فائٹر
FIREFIGHTER
FIREFIGHTER

مالی
MAALI
GARDENER

وكيل
WAKEEL
LAWYER

پائلٹ
PILOT
PILOT

اداكار
ADAKAAR
ACTOR

دندان ساز
DANDAN SAAZ
DENTIST

مكينک
MECHANIC
MECHANIC

صفائی والا
SAFAI WALA
DUSTMAN

محاسب
MUHASIB
ACCOUNTANT

مابر نفسيات
MAAHIR E NAFSIAT
PSYCHOLOGIST

ملازمت
mulazmat

job

صحافی	بڑھئی	موسیقار
SAHAAFI	**BARHAYI**	**MOSIQAR**
JOURNALIST	CARPENTER	MUSICIAN

پلمبر	باورچی	لکھاری
PLUMBER	**BAWARCHI**	**LIKHARI**
PLUMBER	COOK	WRITER

حجام	سیکرٹری	ڈرائیور
HAJJAM	**SECRETARY**	**DRIVER**
HAIRDRESSER	SECRETARY	DRIVER

پولیس اہلکار	طبیب	جانوروں کا ڈاکٹر
POLICE AHALKAR	**TABEEB**	**JANWARON KA DOCTOR**
POLICEMAN	DOCTOR	VETERINARIAN

عینک ساز	بچوں کا ڈاکٹر	ویٹر
AINAK SAZ	**BACHOUN KA DOCTOR**	**WAITER**
OPTICIAN	PEDIATRICIAN	WAITER

آلوبخارہ
Aalu Bukhara
PLUM

آڑو
Aarhu
PEACH

چیری
Cherry
CHERRY

سیب
Saib
APPLE

انگور
Angoor
GRAPE

تربوز
Tarbooz
WATERMELON

اننّاس
Anannaas
PINEAPPLE

اسٹرابیری
Strawberry
STRAWBERRY

رس بھری
Ras Bhari
RASPBERRY

ناشپاتی
Nashpati
PEAR

کیلا
Kela
BANANA

خربوزہ
Kharbooza
MELON

لیموں
Lemoo
LEMON

بلیک بیری
Blackberry
BLACKBERRY

کینو
Keenu
ORANGE

مشروم

Mashroom

MUSHROOM

گوبھی کا پھول

Ghobi ka phool

BROCCOLI

بند گوبھی

Band gobhi

CABBAGE

مارچوبا

Maar Choba

ASPARAGUS

کھیرا

Kheera

CUCUMBER

گاجر

Gaajar

CARROT

مولی

Mooli

RADISH

سلاد کے پتے

Sallad pata

LETTUCE

آلو

Aalo

POTATO

ٹماٹر

Timatar

TOMATO

ایواکاڈو

Avocado

AVOCADO

گندنا

Gandna

LEEK

چقندر

Chukandar

BEETROOT

بینگن

Began

EGGPLANT

آرٹچوک

Artichoke

ARTICHOKE

پرسکون
Pur sukoon
Calm

خوش
Khush
Happy

مایوس
Mayoos
Disappointed

جوشیلا
Josheelaa
Excited

خوفزدہ
Khof Zadha
Frightened

بدمزاج
Bad Mizaj
Grumpy

محبت میں
Muhabbat mein
In Love

حیران
Heran
Surprised

شرمیلا
Sharmeela
Shy

فخر
Fakhar
Proud

غصہ
Gussa
Angry

الجھن میں
Uljhan mein
Confused

تھکا ہارا
Thaka Haara
Tired

گھبراہٹ
Ghabrahat
Nervous

متجسس
Mustajassus
Curious

احساسات
ehsasaat

feelings

		English
لاجواب	lajawab	fantastic
عجیب و غریب	ajeeb o ghareeb	weird
سخت	sakht	hard
مزاحیہ	mazhiya	funny
عجیب	ajeeb	strange
آسان	asaan	easy
ناممکن	namumkin	impossible
جوان	jawaan	young
درست	durust	correct
فارغ	farigh	free
بیمار	bimar	sick
ایک جیسا	ek jesa	same
غریب	ghareeb	poor
ممکن	mumkin	possible
صاف	saaf	clean

صفت
sift

adjectives

گندا	mela	dirty
سادہ	sada	simple
اداس	udaas	sad
خالی	khaali	empty
اچھا	acha	good
نرم	naram	soft
غلط	ghalat	false
بڑا	bara	big
بُرا	bura	bad
سنجیدہ	sanjeeda	serious
پرانا	purana	old
سچ	sach	true
خوبصورت	khoobsoorat	beautiful
گرم	garam	hot
ٹھنڈا	thandaa	cold

مہنگا	mahengaa	expensive
صاف	saaf	clear
آخری	akhri	last
مختلف	mukhtalif	different
مضبوط	mazboot	strong
اچھا	acha	nice
اونچا	oonchaa	high
انسان	insaan	human
ضروری	zaroori	important
دلکش	dilkash	pretty
ہلکا	halka	light
چھوٹا	chota	small
نیا	naya	new
مکمل	mukammal	full
پہلا	pehla	first

گھاس
Ghaas
Grass

کیڑے
Keeray
Insect

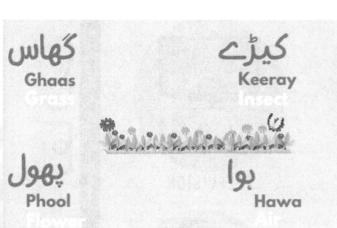

پھول
Phool
Flower

ہوا
Hawa
Air

برف
Baraf
Snow

پہاڑ
Pahar
Mountain

بادل
Badal
Cloud

آسمان
Aasman
Sky

دھند
Dhund
Fog

سمندر
Samandar
Sea

جھیل
Jheel
Lake

ساحل سمندر
Sahil E Samandar
Beach

سورج
Sooraj
Sun

جنگل
Jangal
Forest

درخت
Darakht
Tree

اخبار
Akhbaar
NEWSPAPER

فلم گھر
Film ghar
CINEMA

ٹیلی ویژن
Teli Wisan
TELEVISION

کتاب
Kitab
BOOK

مجسمہ
Mujasma
SCULPTURE

فوٹو گرافی
Photography
PHOTOGRAPHY

موسیقی
Moseeqi
MUSIC

کنسرٹ
Concert
CONCERT

مووی
Movie
MOVIE

کمپیوٹر
Computer
COMPUTER

لغت
Lughat
DICTIONARY

پینٹنگ
Painting
PAINTING

عجائب گھر
Ajaaeb Ghar
MUSEUM

اوپیرا
Opera
OPERA

تھیٹر
Thetar
THEATER

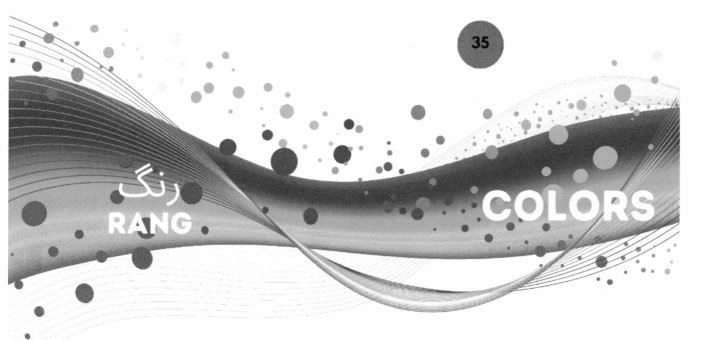

رنگ
RANG

COLORS

نیلا neela	blue	سیاہ siyah	**black**
جامنی jamni	purple	سفید safaid	white
گلابی gulabi	pink	بھورا bhoora	brown
لال laal	red	سونہری sunehri	gold
نارنجی narangi	orange	سرمئی surmai	gray
پیلا peela	yellow	چاندی chaandi	silver
سبز sabz	green	قوس و قزاح qous o quzah	rainbow

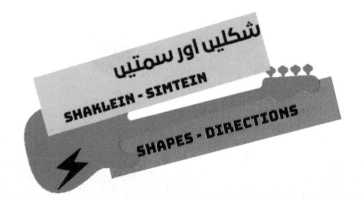

آگے	agay	in front of
پیچھے	peechay	behind
بائیں	bain	left
دائیں	dayin	right
درمیان	darmiyan	middle
چوکور	chakor	square
دائرہ	daira	circle
مستطیل	mastatil	rectangle
مکعب	mokaab	cube
ڈائمنڈ	shakal moueen	diamond
لکیر	lakeer	line
مغرب	maghrib	west
مشرق	mashriq	east
شمال	shumal	north
جنوب	junoob	south

باورچی خانہ
BAAWARCHI KHANA
KITCHEN

دروازہ
DARWAAZAA
DOOR

کھانے کا کمرہ
KHANY KA KAMRA
DINING ROOM

غسل خانہ
GHUSAL KHANAH
BATHROOM

کھڑکی
KHIRKI
WINDOW

سیڑھیاں
SEERHIYAAN
STAIRS

بالا خانہ
BALA KHANA
ATTIC

ہال
HAAL
HALL

دفتر
DAFTAR
OFFICE

بالکونی
BALCONY
BALCONY

تہ خانہ
TEH KHANAH
BASEMENT

پڑوسی
PAROSI
NEIGHBOR

باغ
BAAGH
GARDEN

آرام گاہ
AARAAM GAAH
BEDROOM

اوون OVEN	ریڈی ایٹر RADIATOR	صوفہ SOFA	فرج FRIDGE
OVEN	RADIATOR	SOFA	FRIDGE

چراغ CHARAAGH	بیسن BISAN	ٹیلی فون TELEPHONE	گلاس GLASS
LAMP	SINK	TELEPHONE	GLASS

رکابی RIKAABI	أئینہ AINAA	گھڑی GHARI	کرسی KURSI
PLATE	MIRROR	CLOCK	CHAIR

بیڈ BED	میز MAIZ
BED	TABLE

دیوار
DEWAAR
WALL

چھت
CHAT
ROOF

فریزر
FREEZER
FREEZER

الماری
ALMARI
CUPBOARD

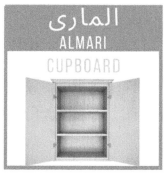

پودا
PODA
PLANT

چمنی
CHIMNI
FIREPLACE

ویکیوم کلینر
VACUUM CLEANER
VACUUM CLEANER

ٹوٹی
TOTI
TAP

ڈش واشر
DISHWASHER
DISHWASHER

مائکروویو
MICROWAVE
MICROWAVE

قالین
QAALEEN
CARPET

گھنٹی
GHANTI
DOORBELL

شٹر
SHUTTER
SHUTTER

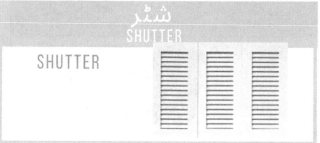

چابی
CHAABI
KEY

تولیہ
TOLIYA
TOWEL

بستر کی چادر
BISTAR KI CHAADAR
BED SHEET

صابن
SABON
SOAP

کنگھی
KANGHI
COMB

پردہ
PARDAA
CURTAIN

کپ
CUP
CUP

شاور
SHOWER
SHOWER

لائٹ بلب
LIGHT BULB
LIGHTBULB

کانٹا
KAANTA
FORK

چمچہ
CHAMCHA
SPOON

چھری
CHURI
KNIFE

باتھ ٹب
BATHTUB
BATHTUB

بوتل
BOTAL
BOTTLE

کوڑے دان
KURAY DAN
GARBAGE CAN

حرفِ جار
harf e jaar

prepositions

کے لیے	kay liyay	for
بعد میں	baad mein	after
پہلے	pehlay	before
کے ساتھ	ka saath	with
بارے میں	baaray mein	about
خلاف	khalaaf	against
میں	main	in
بغیر	bagair	without
جب سے	jab say	since
ارد گرد	ird gird	around
پر	per	on
جیسا	jaisa	like
دوران	doraan	during
درمیان	darmiyan	between
سے	say	from

انسان
Insaan

42

Human

جسم jism body	سر sar head	ہاتھ hath hand

بال baal hair	چہرہ chehra face	انگلی ungli finger

کان kaan ear	آنکھیں ankhein eyes	ناخن nakhun nail

ناک naak nose	منہ muhn mouth	ٹانگ taang leg

دانت daant tooth	ہونٹ hont lips	پاؤں paon foot

انسان
Insaan

43

Human

دماغ
dimagh
brain

خون
khoon
blood

دل
dil
heart

معدہ
meda
stomach

جگر
jigar
liver

گردہ
gurda
kidney

پھپھڑے
phiphray
lungs

آنت
aant
intestine

ناف
naaf
navel

c

کندھا
kandha
shoulder

زبان
zubaan
tongue

پیٹ
pait
belly

کولہا
kulha
hip

گھٹنا
ghutna
knee

ٹخنہ
takhna
ankle

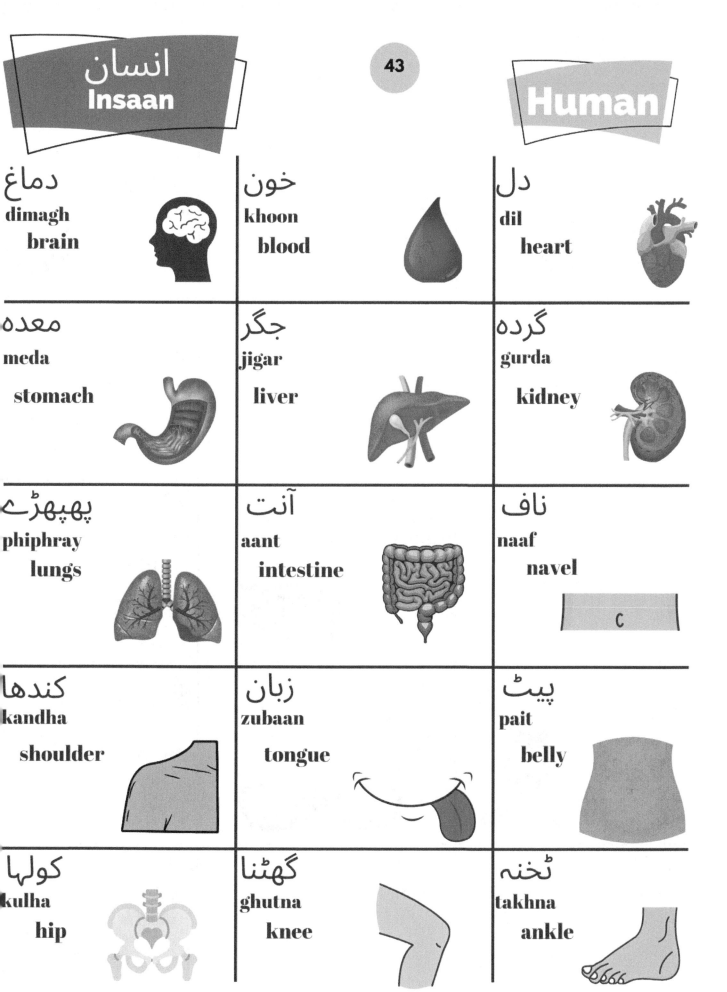

جلد
jild
skin

ہڈی
haddi
bone

کھوپڑی
khopri
skull

گردن
gardan
neck

کلائی
kalai
wrist

بھنویں
bha'nwain
eyebrow

گلا
gala
throat

پپوٹا
papota
eyelid

ٹھوڑی
thori
chin

ڈاڑھی
dari
beard

مونچھ
moonchh
mustache

پٹھا
patha
muscle

کُہنی
kuhni
elbow

انگوٹھا
angotha
toe

گال
gaal
cheek

گزشتہ روز	guzishta roz	yesterday
آج	aaj	today
آنے والا کل	anay wala kal	tomorrow
ابھی	abhi	now
جلد	jald	soon
دیر	der	late
یہاں	yahan	here
فاصلہ	fasla	distance
طلوع آفتاب	tulu aftab	sunrise
دوپہر	dopehar	noon
شام	shaam	evening
آدھی رات	aadhi raat	midnight
دہائی	dahai	decade
صدی	sadi	century
ہزار سال	hazar saal	millennium

یورپ
Europe

Europe

افریقہ
Africa

Africa

ایشیاء
Asia

Asia

امریکہ
Amrika

America

انگلینڈ
England

England

جرمنی
Germany

Germany

فرانس
France

France

اسپین
Spain

Spain

اٹلی
Italy

Italy

ریاستہائے امریکہ
Riasathae Amrika

United States

برازیل
Brazil

Brazil

جاپان
Japan

Japan

چین
Cheen

China

بھارت
Bharat

India

روس
Roose

Russia

میکسیکو
Macsico

Mexico

مِصر
Misar

Egypt

تُرکی
Turki

Turkey

نائیجیریا
Nigeria

Nigeria

تھائی لینڈ
Thai Land

Thailand

جنوبی کوریا
Janoobi Korea

South Korea

کولمبیا
Kolambia

Colombia

ارجنٹینا
Argentina

Argentina

الجیریا
Aljirya

Algeria

پولینڈ
Poland

Poland

سعودی عرب
Saudi Arab

Saudi Arabia

کیمرون
Cameroon

Cameroon

نیدرلینڈز
Netherlands

Netherlands

سوئٹزرلینڈ
Switzerland

Switzerland

سویڈن
Swedan

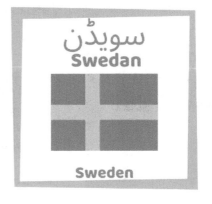

Sweden

يونان
Yunan

Greece

بیلجیم
Belgium

Belgium

آئرلینڈ
Ireland

Ireland

ناروے
Norway

Norway

آسٹریلیا
Austrelia

Australia

ڈنمارک
Denmark

Denmark

آسٹریا
Ostria

Austria

فن لینڈ
Finland

Finland

پرتگال
Portugal

Portugal

جنوبی افریقہ
Janoobi Afrika

South Africa

انڈونیشیا
Indonesia

Indonesia

تنزانیہ
Tanznia

Tanzania

یوکرین
Ukraine

Ukraine

پیرو
Pairo

Peru

چلّی
Chille

Chile

ملک

MULAK

COUNTRY

اُردو

يورپی
Europi

European

امریکی
Ameriki

American

انگریزی
Angraizi

English

فرانسیسی
Francisi

French

ہسپانوی
Hapanvi

Spanish

اطالوی
Atalvi

Italien

جرمن
German

German

افریقی
Afriki

African

ایشیائی
Aishiyai

Asian

روسی
Russi

Russian

چینی
Cheni

Chinese

کینیڈین
Canadien

Canadien

ہندوستانی
Hindustani

Indian

برازیلین
Brazilian

Brazilian

میکسیکن
Mexican

Mexican

ABADI

POPULATION

پتلون
Patloon
Pants

ٹائی
Tai
Tie

قمیض
Kameez
Shirt

موزے
Mozay
Socks

جیکٹ
Jacket
Jacket

چشمے
Chashmy
Glasses

جوتے
Jotay
Shoes

لباس
Libas
Dress

بیلٹ
Belt
Belt

ٹوپی
Topi
Hat

پرس
Purse
Wallet

چھتری
Chhatri
Umbrella

ٹوپی
Topi
Beanie

دوپٹہ
Dupatta
Scarf

دستانے
Dastany
Gloves

کڑا	گھڑی	زیورات
KARRA	**GHARI**	**ZEWARAAT**
BRACELET	WATCH	JEWELRY

انگوٹھی	بالیاں	رومال
ANGOTHI	**BALIYAAN**	**ROMAAL**
RING	EARRINGS	HANDKERCHIEF

پاجامے	سینڈل	جوتے
PAJAMAY	**SANDALS**	**JUTAY**
PAJAMAS	SANDALS	BOOTS

تسمے	ہار	چپل
TASMAY	**HAAR**	**CHAPAL**
SHOELACE	NECKLACE	SLIPPERS

میک اپ	ہینڈ بیگ	جیب
MAKE UP	**HANDBAG**	**JAIB**
MAKEUP	HANDBAG	POCKET

كائنات
Kainat
Universe

کہکشاں
Kehkashaan
Galaxy

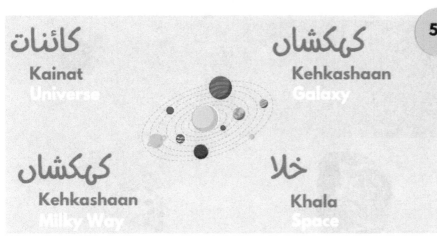

کہکشاں
Kehkashaan
Milky Way

خلا
Khala
Space

دُم دار تارا
Dum Dar Tara
Comet

سیارچہ
Syarcha
Asteroid

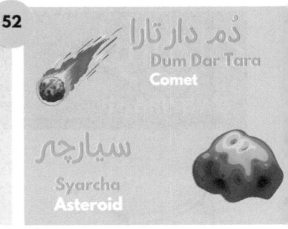

چاند
Chand
Moon

زمین
Zameen
Earth

ستارہ
Sitara
Star

وقت
Waqt
Time

روشنی
Roshani
Light

سیارہ
Sayarah
Planet

خلاباز
Khala Baaz
Astronaut

راکٹ
Raket
Rocket

سیٹلائٹ
Satellite
Satellite

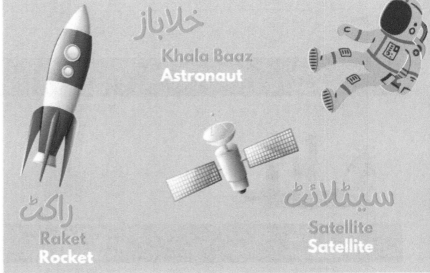

قیمت

Keemat
Price

ادائیگی کرنا

Adaigy Karna
To pay

پیسے

Paisay
Money

گاہک

Gahak
Client

تحفہ

Tuhfa
Gift

آن لائن

Online
Online

بینک

Bank
Bank

بک اسٹور

Bookstore
Bookstore

دواخانہ

Dawa khana
Pharmacy

سٹور

Store
Store

ریسٹورنٹ

Restaurant
Restaurant

پارٹی

Party
Party

شادی

Shadi
Wedding

پیدائش

Paidaish
Birth

سالگرہ

Saal gira
Birthday

53

متعلق فعل
mutaliq fail

adverbs

ہمیشہ	hamesha	always
کہیں اور	kahin or	elsewhere
تقریباً	takreeban	approximately
ہر جگہ	harjagah	everywhere
کہیں	kahin	somewhere
کہیں بھی	kahinbhi	anywhere
کہیں نہیں	kahin nahi	nowhere
اندر	andr	inside
باہر	bahir	outside
اس طرح	istrah	thus
قریب	qareeb	near
اوپر	oper	above
آہستہ آہستہ	ahista ahista	slowly
فوراً	foran	quickly
واقعی	waqai	really

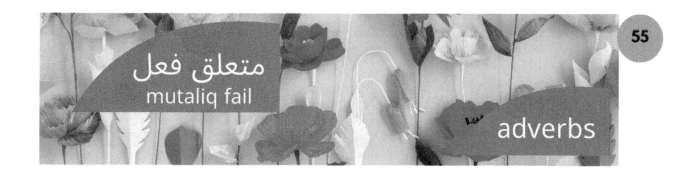

متعلق فعل
mutaliq fail

adverbs

فقط	faqt	simply
سنجیدگی سے	sanjidgi sy	seriously
خوش قسمتی سے	khush qismati sy	fortunately
کبھی کبھار	kabhi kabhar	sometimes
شاذ و نادر ہی	shaz o nadir hi	rarely
کافی	kafi	enough
سب سے پہلے	sb sy pehly	firstly
پہلے	pehly	before
بعد میں	baad mein	after
البتہ	albata	however
کبھی نہیں	kabhi nahi	never
حال ہی میں	haal hi mein	recently
پھر	phir	then
اکثر	aksar	often
عام طور پر	aam tor pr	usually

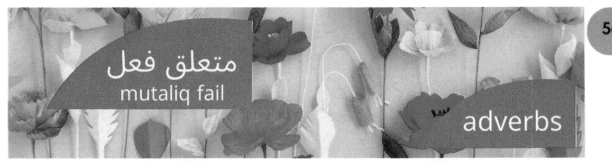

متعلق فعل
mutaliq fail

adverbs

بہتر	behtar	better
اچھا	acha	well
بہت زیادہ	bohat zyada	a lot
بلکہ	balkay	rather
بہت	bohat	quite
تو	tou	so
بھی	bhi	too
تھوڑا	thorha	little
دور	door	far
بہت زیادہ	bohat zyada	very
تقریباً	taqriban	almost
پہلے سے	pehlay say	already
جب سے	jab say	since
اچانک	achaanak	suddenly
واقعی	waqai	indeed

ننھا بچہ
Nanna bachcha
Baby

بچہ
Bachcha
Child

لڑکا
Larka
Boy

لڑکی
Larki
Girl

نوعمر
No umer
Teenager

عورت
Oarat
Woman

آدمی
Aadmi
Man

بالغ
Baligh
Adult

دوست
Dost
Friend

کزن
Kazan
Cousin

ساتھی
Saathi
Colleague

محبت
Muhabat
Love

دوستی
Dosti
Friendship

خوشی
Khushi
Happiness

خوشی
Khushi
Joy

ٹیم
TEAM

TEAM

کھلاڑی
KHILARI

PLAYER

اسٹیڈیم
STADIUM

STADIUM

فٹ بال
FOOTBALL

FOOTBALL/SOCCER

ریفری
REFRI

REFEREE

گیند
GAIND

BALL

جرسی
JERSI

JERSEY

تربیت
TARBIYT

TRAINING

درجہ بندی
DRJA BANDI

RANKING

گھڑسواری
GHORD SAWARI

HORSE RIDING

سائیکلنگ
CYCLING

CYCLING

تیراکی
TYRAKI

SWIMMING

کوچ
COACH

COACH

چوٹ
CHOOT

INJURY

ٹریک اور فیلڈ
TRACK AND FIELD

TRACK AND FIELD

حکومت
Hakomat
Government

صدر
Sadar
President

میئر
Mayar
Mayor

سیاست
Siyasat
Politics

دنیا
Dunya
World

ملک
Mulk
Country

لوگ
Log
People

براعظم
Barazam
Continent

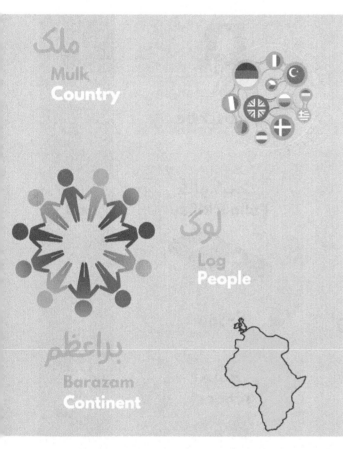

شہر
Shehar
City

شہر
Shehar
Town

پارک
Park
Park

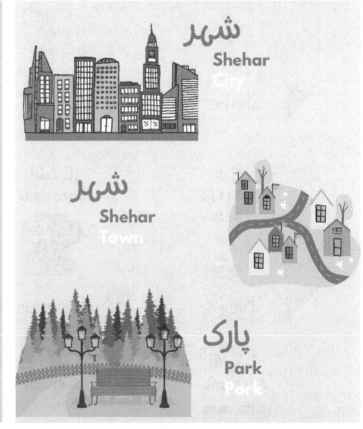

کمپنی
Campany
Company

جزیرہ
Jazera
Island

صحرا
Sehra
Desert

بسپتال
Hasptaal
Hospital

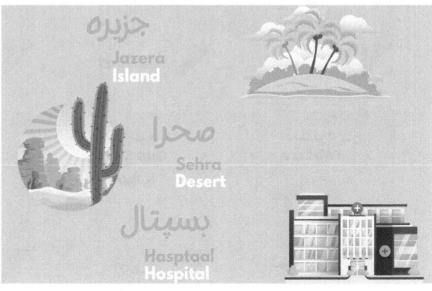

سماجی رابطے
Samaji Rabty

Social network

صارف
Sarif

User

شائع کرنا
Shaya krna

Publish

بانٹنا
Bantana

Share

مواد
Muwaad

Content

سبسکرائب
Subscribe

Subscribe

خبریں
Khabrain

News

اشتہار
Ishtehaar

Advertising

فالو کیجئے
Follow Kijiay

Follow

اکاونٹ
Account

Account

چینل
Chennal

Channel

تحقیق
Tehqeek

Research

تبصرہ
Tabsara

Comment

گپ شپ
Gup Shup

Chat

لنک
Link

Link

کی بورڈ **kiboard** Keyboard	لیپ ٹاپ **Laptop** Laptop	نیٹ ورک **Network** Network
پاسورڈ **Password** Password	پرنٹر **Printer** Printer	سکرین **Screen** Screen
تار **Tar** Cable	کنٹرولر **Kantroller** Controller	ڈاؤن لوڈ کریں **Download karin** Download
ائیر فون **Ear phone** Earphones	کیلکولیٹر **Calculator** Calculator	یو ایس بی فلیش ڈرائیو **USB Flash Drive** USB Flash Drive
ویڈیو گیمز **Video Games** Video games	سافٹ ویئر **Software** Software	فائل **File** File

مسئلہ	masla	problem
خیال	khiyal	idea
سوال	sawal	question
جواب	jawab	answer
سوچ	soch	thought
روح	rooh	spirit
آغاز	aghaz	beginning
اختتام	ikhtitaam	end
قانون	qanoon	law
زندگی	zindagi	life
موت	moat	death
امن	aman	peace
خاموشی	khamoshi	silence
خواب	khawab	dream
وزن	wazan	weight

رائے raye	opinion
چیز cheez	thing
غلطی ghalti	mistake
بھوک bhook	hunger
پیاس piyas	thirst
انتخاب intakhab	choice
طاقت takat	strength
تصویر tasweer	picture
روبوٹ roboot	robot
جھوٹ jhoot	lie
سچ sach	truth
شور shoor	noise
کچھ نہیں kuch nahi	nothing
سب کچھ sab kuch	everything
نصف nisaf	half

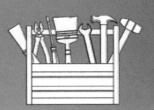

کلھاڑی **KULHARI** AXE	ڈرل **DRILL** DRILL	گوند **GOND** GLUE

بتھوڑا **HATHORA** HAMMER	سیڑھی **SEHRI** LADDER	کیل **KEEL** NAIL

پیچ کَس **PAICH KASS** SCREWDRIVER	ریک **REAK** RAKE	گھاس کاٹنے کی مشین **GHAS KATNY KI MACHINE** MOWER

آرا **ARA** SAW	گَتا **GATTA** CARDBOARD	ہتھ ریڑھی **HATH RERHI** WHEELBARROW

پانی والا کین **PANI WALA CAN** WATERING CAN	پیچ **PAECH** SCREW	بیلچہ **BELCHA** SHOVEL

الرجی	allergy	allergy
زکام	zukam	flu
آرام	araam	rest
علاج	ilaaj	medication
ویکسین	vaccine	vaccine
اینٹی بائیوٹک	antibiotic	antibiotic
بخار	bukhar	fever
صحت مند ہو جانا	sehat mand ho jana	heal
صحت	sehat	health
انفیکشن	infection	infection
علامت	alamat	symptom
متعدی	mutaadi	contagious
بیماری	bimaari	sickness
درد	dard	pain
کھانسی	khansi	cough

ایٹم
Atom
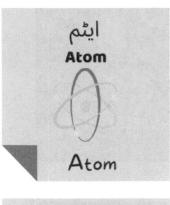
Atom

جرثومہ
Jarsooma
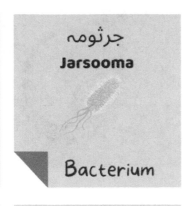
Bacterium

خُلیہ
Khulia
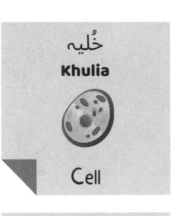
Cell

کیمیا
Kimiya

Chemistry

حیاتیات
Hayatiyat

Biology

خوردبین
Khordbeen

Microscope

مالیکیول
Molecule
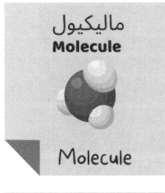
Molecule

حساب
Hisaab
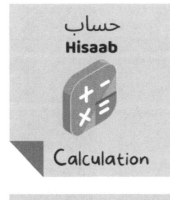
Calculation

نتیجہ
Nateeja

Result

جمع
Jama

Addition

منفی
Manfi

Subtraction

تقسیم
Takseem

Division

ضرب
Zarb

Multiplication

قوسین
Qosain

Parenthesis

فیصد
Fee Sad

Percentage

جامعہ
JAMEA
UNIVERSITY

کارخانہ
KARKHANA
FACTORY

عمارت
AMAARAT
BUILDING

جیل
JAIL
JAIL

ٹاؤن ہال
TOWN HALL
TOWN HALL

پُل
PUL
BRIDGE

قلعہ
QILA
CASTLE

قبرستان
KABRISTAAN
CEMETERY

فوارہ
FAWARA
FOUNTAIN

سرنگ
SURANG
TUNNEL

چڑیا گھر
CHIRIYA GHAR
ZOO

عدالت
ADALAT
COURT

سرکس
CIRCUS
CIRCUS

رقص گاہ
RAQS GAH
CASINO

لیبارٹری
LABORTARY
LABORATORY

روئی Roi  Cotton	لکڑی Lakri  Wood	اینٹ Eent  Brick
کنکریٹ Concret  Concrete	اُون Oon  Wool	چمڑہ Chamra  Leather
دھات Dhaat  Metal	سنگِ مرمر Sang e marmar  Marble	فولاد Folaad  Steel
چینی کے برتن Cheeni kay bartan  Porcelain	گارا Gara  Clay	پلاسٹک Plastic  Plastic
ربڑ Rubber  Rubber	کاغذ Kagiz  Paper	ریت Rait  Sand

MAWAAD

MATERIALS

زمین
Zameen

Earth

زلزلہ
zalzala
earthquake

آگ
aag
fire

کھیت
khait
field

برفانی تودہ
barfani toda
avalanche

طوفان
toofan
tornado

چٹان
chatan
cliff

سمندر
samadar
ocean

آتش فشاں
aatish fishan
volcano

ریت کا ٹیلہ
rait ka teela
dune

لہر
lehar
wave

پہاڑ
pahaar
hill

برف کا تودہ
barf ka toda
glacier

جنگل
jangal
jungle

وادی
wadi
valley

غار
ghaar
cave

آرکسٹرا
ORCHESTRA
ORCHESTRA

گانا
GANA
SONG

موسیقار
MOSIKAR
MUSICIAN

گٹار
GUITAR
GUITAR

گلوکار
GULUKAAR
SINGER

پیانو
PIANO
PIANO

ڈھول
DHOL
DRUMS

سارنگی
SARANGI
VIOLIN

ترم
TARAM
TRUMPET

گانے کے بول
GANY KE BOL
LYRICS

سامعین
SAMAEEN
AUDIENCE

آواز
AWAZ
VOICE

مائیکروفون
MICROPHONE
MICROPHONE

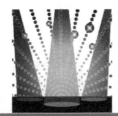

چبوترا
CHABOOTRA
STAGE

والیم
VOLUME
VOLUME

پتہ
Pata
Address

ڈاک
Dak
Mail

لفافہ
Lifafa
Envelope

ڈاک ٹکٹ
Dak Ticket
Stamp

ڈاک بکس
Dak Box
Mailbox

بل
Bill
Bill

بجلی
Bijli
Electricity

گیس
Gas
Gas

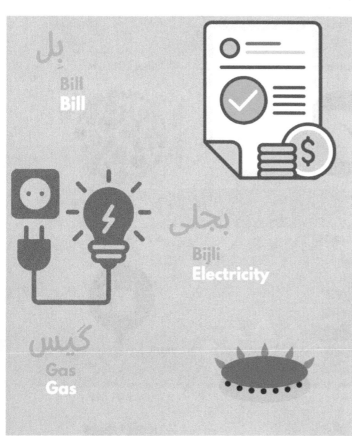

تنخواہ
Tankhua
Salary

سبسکرپشن
Subscription
Subscription

پیکج
Package
Package

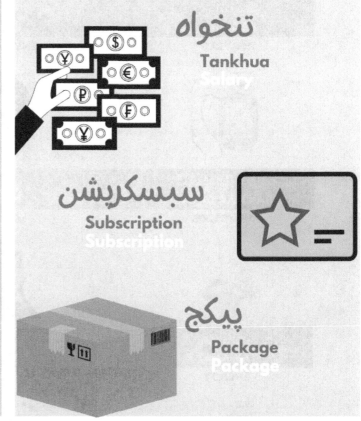

ڈاکیا
Dakiya
Postman

بھیجنا
Bhejna
Send

بیچنا
Bechna
Sell

خریدنا
Khareedna
Buy

ری سائیکل	ماحول	آلودگی
RECYCLE	**MAHOLE**	**ALOODGI**
RECYCLE	ENVIRONMENT	POLLUTION

کیڑے مار دوائیں	نامیاتی	سبزی خور
KEERAY MAR DAWAIN	**NAMIATI**	**SABZI KHOR**
PESTICIDES	ORGANIC	VEGETARIAN

توانائی	کوئلہ	گیسولین
TAWANAI	**KOYLA**	**GASOLINE**
ENERGY	COAL	GASOLINE

جوہری	ماحولیاتی نظام	کسی خطہ کے جانور
JOHARI	**MAHOLITI NIZAM**	**KISI KHITTA KE JANWAR**
NUCLEAR	ECOSYSTEM	FAUNA

نباتیات	درجہ حرارت	قطب شمالی
NIBATIAAT	**DARJA HARARAT**	**QUTUB SHUMALI**
FLORA	TEMPERATURE	ARCTIC